IN A GLASS

IN A GLASS

Francis van Arkel

NEW
HOLLAND

Published in 2012 by New Holland Publishers
London • Sydney • Auckland • Cape Town
www.newhollandpublishers.com
www.newholland.com.au

Garfield House 86–88 Edgware Road London W2 2EA United Kingdom
1/66 Gibbes Street Chatswood NSW 2067 Australia
218 Lake Road Northcote Auckland New Zealand
Wembley Square First Floor Solan Road Gardens Cape Town 8001 South Africa

First published by Veltman Uitgevers as *Amuses in Glassjes*
Copyright © 2012 New Holland Publishers

ISBN 9781742573441

Text, recipes and food styling: Francis van Arkel, NutriVisie
Styling: Moniek Visser
Photography: Remco Lassche (Bart Nijs Fotografie)
Translation: Textcase Utrecht
Design: Tracy Loughlin, Stephanie Foti
Production Director: Olga Dementiev
Printed by Toppan Leefung (China) Ltd

10 9 8 7 6 5 4 3 2 1
Follow New Holland Publishers on Facebook: www.facebook.com/NewHollandPublishers

CONTENTS

FOREWORD

There are endless ways you can present and fill your glasses to enhance every dinner party or event with a little bite.

These bite-size tasters can be served before or with one of the courses during a meal. In more expensive restaurants, it is quite common to serve a small *amuse*, or dish in a glass, before the starter, allowing the kitchen to show guests what they can expect from the meal. The *amuse* can be seen as a type of foreplay to the culinary climaxes that are still to come!

As you welcome guests for dinner, many entertainers serve an *amuse* before the meal, especially if they are organising a festive dinner party. *Amuses* are eaten at the table and are easy to eat. They should indeed 'amuse the mouth': just a small tasty bite that makes your guests hungry for more.

The recipes in this book all make eight *amuses*. If you do have a party of 4 to cook for, simply halve the recipe.

Besides the *amuses* you can serve before the meal, we also created some *amuses* that can be served as a dessert. This phenomenon is becoming more and more popular in restaurants as well. These *amuses* 'cleanse' the palate, to prepare your mouth for the sweet dessert that is to follow.

Of course, you may find that one or more of the *amuses* in this book are so nice you just can't stop eating them. Then just go ahead and turn the *amuse* into a fully-fledged starter. Just double or triple the ingredients for the recipe. Serve the *amuse* with a salad or on a larger plate, with some freshly baked bread, and you have a lovely starter to wow your guests!

Francis van Arkel

INTRODUCTION

This book shows you how to to create *amuses*, which can be served as a taster before a larger meal. The *amuses* are refined and tasty, and stimulate your appetite. That is exactly what an *amuse* is meant to do; especially in combination with an aperitif—with or without alcohol—to activate our taste buds. It makes your guest hungry for more.

When you are cooking your own meal at home, make sure you select an *amuse* that fits with the rest of your menu.

Your guests will be surprised when you serve an *amuse*, preferably with a nice apéritif, such as a glass of wine or some fresh fruit juice. It is the perfect way to start a dinner party. The *amuse* will not only get your guests talking, but they will start wondering what else you will be serving up.

The glassware

Presentation is extremely important when it comes to *amuses*. It is the first thing a guest is presented with. An *amuse* should be small but delicate, both to see and eat. Garnish your *amuse* with a curly fry, a bit of green or some lemon peel. You can also drizzle over a bit of sauce or dressing or sprinkle over some finely chopped herbs.

There are many types of beautiful glasses you can buy in stores, in all shapes and sizes. Any glasses you have will work, even if your glasses are a bit larger than the ones I used in this book. Just make sure you don't fill them up too much.

Want to use something else?

Do you want to serve your *amuse* in something other than a glass? Let your own creativity run wild! There are plenty of ways to present these little bites.

You can use spoons for mousse or small cuts of meat or fish. You can also use a small plate or a small dish or bowl. You can stack the various tastes and construct a small tower. There are also special *amuse* forks, which are perfect for a slice of smoked duck breast drizzled with sauce and of course garnished with a bit of green.

SOUP IN A GLASS

SEAFOOD SOUP

SERVES 8

Heat the olive oil in a pan and sauté the seafood with the onion, carrot and leek for a couple of minutes.

Add the tomato puree and let it cook for a minute.

Add the wine and the sherry. Pour in enough water to cover everything. Stir in the salt and let the seafood and vegetable simmer for 30 minutes.

Strain the soup through a sieve, pour back in the pan and let it reduce, to concentrate the flavours. Add the cream and foam up the soup with a blender.

Divide the shrimps over the preheated glasses and pour over the soup. Garnish the soup with radish sprout.

300 g (10½ oz) seafood (shrimps (prawns), langoustine, lobster etc.)
4 tbsp olive oil
½ onion, cut into wedges
½ carrot, cut into pieces
½ leek, cut into pieces
½ tin of tomato puree
100 ml (3½ fl oz) dry white wine
a dash of sherry
100 ml (3½ fl oz) whipping cream
125 g (4 oz) small shrimps (prawns)
salt

WITLOF SOUP WITH SHREDDED HAM

SERVES 8

Heat the olive oil in a pan and cook the onion and witlof on a low heat for 10 minutes. Pour in the stock and leave the soup to simmer for 20 minutes.

Puree the soup with the cream in the food processor or with the blender, and add salt and pepper to taste.

Divide the soup over the glasses. Cut the remaining witlof leaves into strips and mix these up with the ham and cress. Sprinkle this over the soup and garnish the soup with a witlof leaf.

1 tbsp olive oil

1 onion, shredded

3 heads of witlof, washed and cut into strips (keep a few leaves whole)

400 ml (14 fl oz) chicken stock (fresh or made from a stock cube)

100 ml (3½ fl oz) whipping cream

50 g (1¾ oz) ham strips, chopped

a few sprigs of garden cress

salt and pepper

GAZPACHO WITH RED ONION

SERVES 8

Soak the bread in the wine. Puree the softened bread, the tomatoes, cucumber, bell pepper, chilli pepper, garlic and salt in the food processor or with a blender. Add the oil and vinegar.

Taste and add more salt and pepper or vinegar if necessary. Keep into account that the flavours will intensify. Strain the soup through a sieve and put it in the fridge for a few hours to chill and to let the flavours infuse.

Taste the soup and season to taste. Divide the soup over the glasses and sprinkle with the red onion and parsley.

2 slices of white bread

3–4 tbsp red wine

250 g (9 oz) tomatoes, skinned and cut into pieces

¼ peeled cucumber, deseeded and cut into pieces

¼ red bell pepper (capsicum), cut into pieces

2 cloves of garlic, cut into pieces

50 ml (1¾ fl oz) olive oil

½ chilli, deseeded

2–3 tbsp red wine vinegar

½ red onion, shredded

1 tbsp parsley, finely chopped

salt

CURRY CAPPUCCINO

SERVES 8

Pour the port, Noilly Prat and wine in the pan and bring to the boil. Let simmer until the liquids are reduced by half.

Melt the butter in a separate pan and sauté the shallot, leek and apple for a couple of minutes. Add the curry. Let the curry cook for a bit and add the wine liquid. Pour in the stock and the cream and leave this to simmer for 10 minutes.

Puree the soup in the food processor or with a blender. Strain the soup through a sieve and add the grated coconut. Season the soup with tabasco, salt and pepper.

Froth the milk. Divide the soup over the glasses and scoop over the milk froth. Sprinkle over some grated coconut (optional) and garnish with shiso cress.

75 ml (2½ fl oz) white port
75 ml (2½ fl oz) Noilly Prat
75 ml (2½ fl oz) white wine
1 tbsp butter
2 shallots, shredded
1 small leek, only the white, finely chopped
½ apple, finely chopped
1 tbsp curry powder
400 ml (14 fl oz) poultry stock
200 ml (7 fl oz) whipping cream
2 tbsp grated coconut
tabasco
salt and pepper
150 ml (5 fl oz) milk

CHILLED AVOCADO SOUP WITH CRAYFISH TAILS

SERVES 8

Cut the avocado in half, remove the stone and peel it. Cut the avocado flesh in cubes and immediately sprinkle with lemon juice to prevent browning. Puree the avocado, ricotta and crème fraîche in the food processor or with a blender, and add the stock and vermouth. Season the soup with salt and pepper. Chill the soup in the fridge for at least half an hour for the flavours to infuse.

Divide the soup over the glasses and sprinkle over some crumbled goat's cheese and crayfish tails. You can also string the crayfish onto a skewer and put it in the glass. Garnish the soup with some tarragon (optional).

1 ripe avocado
1 tbsp lemon juice
50 g (1¾ oz) ricotta cheese
50 ml (1¾ fl oz) crème fraîche
400 ml (14 fl oz) herb broth (fresh or made from a stock cube)
2 tbsp dry white vermouth
50 g (1¾ oz) soft goat's cheese, crumbled
125 g (4 oz) crayfish tails, or pieces of crayfish
salt and pepper

BEETROOT SOUP WITH HERRING

SERVES 8

Melt the butter in a pan and sauté the carrot, leek and celery for 4–5 minutes. Add the beetroot and let this cook for 2–3 minutes. Pour in the stock and leave the soup to simmer for 10 minutes.

Puree the soup in the food processor or with a blender. Stir in half the herring and season the soup with salt and pepper. Mix the beetroot cubes with the remaining herring and the dill. Divide the soup over the glasses. Spoon over some sour cream and garnish with the herring and beetroot mix.

1 tbsp butter

1 small carrot, cut into pieces

½ leek, cut into pieces

1 celery stick, cut into pieces

2 cooked beetroots, cut into pieces (dice 1 tbsp of beetroot and keep separate)

400 ml (14 fl oz) fish stock (fresh or made from a stock cube)

1 herring, diced

1 tbsp dill, finely chopped

125 ml (4 fl oz) sour cream

Courgette soup with a scallop skewer

Serves 8

Heat the olive oil in a pan and sauté the courgette, garlic and shallot for 3–4 minutes, making sure they don't brown.

Add the stock. Bring to the boil and leave the soup to simmer for 10 minutes until the courgette has softened.

Puree the soup with the dill in the food processor or with a blender and stir in the cream. Season the soup with salt and pepper.

Rub the scallops with the chilli oil and sprinkle over some salt. Fry or grill them for 1–2 minutes in the (griddle) pan, turn, and cook the other side for 1 minute. Push them onto a skewer.

Warm up the glasses and pour in the soup. Sprinkle over some diced courgette and a sprig of dill (optional). Add the scallop skewer, making sure the scallop does not touch the soup. You can also balance the skewer on top of the glass. Garnish the soup with some dill (optional).

2 tbsp olive oil

1 courgette (zucchini), cut into pieces

1 clove of garlic, cut into pieces

1 shallot, cut into pieces

400 ml (14 fl oz) vegetable stock (fresh or made from a stock cube)

100 ml (3½ fl oz) whipping cream

1 bunch of dill, chopped

2 tbsp chilli oil

4 scallops (without the shell)

salt and pepper

VEGETABLES
IN A GLASS

ARTICHOKE PUREE WITH GOAT'S CHEESE

SERVES 8

4 artichokes
lemon juice
1 clove of garlic, finely chopped
4 basil leaves, finely chopped
50 g (1¾ oz) goat's cheese, grated

Rinse the artichokes under the tap and leave them to soak in some water with vinegar or lemon juice, to remove the last bits of debris. Break off the stalks and remove the tough outer leaves. Trim the base so that it sits flush and rub with lemon juice. Cook the artichoke in salted water with some lemon juice for at least 20 minutes. The artichoke is done when the leaves come off easily. Snap off the leaves one by one. The leaves are a lovely succulent treat—you can serve them separately with a nice vinaigrette.

In between the bottom leaves and the base is a fibrous, hairy layer. This layer is not edible and should be removed. We are only using the artichoke hearts.

Puree these with the garlic, basil and goat's cheese. Season with salt and pepper. Strain through a sieve and add lemon juice to taste. Divide the puree over the glasses. Garnish the *amuses* with half an olive, a few artichoke leaves and a basil leaf (optional).

WITLOF SALAD WITH GORGONZOLA, PEAR AND WALNUT

SERVES 8

1 head of witlof (chicory)
1 head of radicchio
25 g (¾ oz) walnuts, chopped
1 pear, not too ripe, in strips
50 g (1¾ oz) gorgonzola, crumbled
1 tbsp white balsamic vinegar
2 tbsp olive oil
2 tbsp parsley, finely chopped

Cut the base of the witlof and loosen the leaves. Keep a few smaller leaves separate and cut the rest into strips. Mix up the witlof with the walnuts, pear and gorgonzola. Season the salad with balsamic vinegar, olive oil, salt and pepper.

Scoop the salad into the glasses. Mix the rest of the witlof leaves with the parsley and use as garnish.

PEA CAVIAR WITH PESTO

SERVES 8

25 g (¾ oz) basil leaves
2 cloves of garlic
50 g (1¾ oz) Parmesan, grated
20 g (²⁄₃ oz) pine nuts, roasted
5–6 tbsp olive oil
200 g (7 oz) cooked peas
1 egg yolk
5 tbsp whipping cream

Puree the basil, garlic, Parmesan, pine nuts and olive oil in the food processor or with a blender until you have a smooth pesto.

Mash the peas with the egg yolk and cream. Stir in 1 spoonful of pesto and fill the glasses. Garnish the *amuse* with a dollop of pesto, Parmesan and basil.

CAULIFLOWER MOUSSE WITH APPLE COMPOTE AND CURRY FOAM

SERVES 8

4 small apples

2 tbsp sugar

100 ml (3½ fl oz) water

1 small cauliflower, cut into
    florets

500 ml (17½ fl oz) chicken stock
    (fresh or made from a stock
    cube)

50 ml (1¾ fl oz) whipping cream

for the curry foam:

100 ml (3½ fl oz) milk

100 ml (3½ fl oz) whipping cream

200 ml (7 fl oz) chicken stock
    (fresh or made from a stock
    cube)

½ tsp curry powder

a few saffron threads

Peel and core the apples and cut into wedges. Bring the water and the sugar to the boil and stew the apples until they're soft. Set the pan in the fridge until chilled.

Pour enough chicken stock on the cauliflower to submerge it. Boil the stock until the cauliflower is nearly cooked. Add the cream and let this reduce a little bit more. Puree the cauliflower in a food processor or with a blender. Make sure there is enough liquid to get a creamy mass. Strain the puree through a sieve.

Heat up the milk, for the foam, with the cream and stock. Add the curry and the saffron, and let this simmer for 10 minutes. Season the curry foam with salt and pepper and strain through a sieve.

Fill up the glasses halfway with the mousse and add a spoonful of apple compote. Heat the curry mixture and froth it up in a milk frother. Add some on top of the compote. Garnish the *amuse* with some lime zest (optional).

LASAGNE WITH SPINACH, RICOTTA AND SAGE BUTTER

SERVES 8

2 tbsp olive oil
1 shallot, shredded
1 clove of garlic, finely chopped
150 g (5 oz) fresh spinach
2 tbsp ricotta cheese
1 tbsp pine nuts, finely chopped
8 fresh lasagne sheets
50 g (1¾ oz) butter
10 sage leaves, finely chopped

Heat the olive oil in a pan and sauté the shallot and garlic for 1–2 minutes. Add the spinach and let it wilt while stirring. Season the spinach with salt and pepper and transfer to a colander to drain off. Drain off as much of the liquid as possible and then finely chop the spinach. Stir in the ricotta and pine nuts.

Cut three small circles from each lasagne sheet and cook these al dente in salted water. Drain the lasagne. Place a lasagne circle in each glass, add a bit of the spinach mixture, followed by another lasagne circle, spinach, lasagne and spinach. Melt the butter over a medium heat and sauté the sage leaves. Make sure the butter doesn't brown. Pour over the lasagne.

Garnish the *amuses* with some parsley and cherry tomatoes (optional).

CANDIED HERBS AND TOMATO CHIPS

SERVES 8

2 firm tomatoes, in thin slices
250 ml (9 fl oz) olive oil
1 sprig of rosemary
1 sprig of thyme
1 clove of garlic, crushed
a few peppercorns, crushed
1 fennel bulb, cored and diced
    (retain the fennel green)
1 carrot, diced
1 small courgette (zucchini or
    cucumber), diced

Arrange the tomato slices in a greased baking tray and let them dry in the oven, preheated to 100°C (200°F), for at least an hour. Turn the tomatoes occasionally. Arrange the dried out tomate slices on kitchen paper, to ensure the last of the liquid is drained off.

Heat the olive oil in a pan. Add the rosemary, thyme, garlic and peppercorns, and let them bubble away for 10 minutes. Add the fennel, carrot and courgette and let all this cook on a low heat for another 15 minutes.

Transfer the vegetables to a colander to drain off. Make sure you catch the drained off oil in a bowl underneath. Remove the rosemary, thyme, garlic and peppercorns, and divide the vegetables over the glasses. Spoon over some of the oil and garnish the amuses with the fennel green and rolled-up tomato chips.

ROCKET MOUSSE WITH COURGETTE OIL

SERVES 8

1 tbsp olive oil
1 shallot, shredded
½ leek, only the white, finely
  chopped
75 g (2½ oz) rocket (arugula),
  coarsely shredded
dash of dry white wine
2 gelatine leaves
125 ml (4 fl oz) whipped cream
100 ml (3½ fl oz) olive oil
¼ small courgette (zucchini),
  finely diced

Heat the olive oil in a pan and sauté the onion and leek for 2–3 minutes. Add the rocket and let this wilt for a few minutes. Deglaze with the white wine and let this reduce a bit. Puree the mixture in a food processor or with a blender and bring back to the boil. Soak the gelatine leaves in a large bowl of cold water for 10 minutes, squeeze them out and stir them in the rocket mixture. Stir in the cream. Season the mousse with salt and pepper and let it cool down.

Divide the mousse over the glasses. Set the glasses in the fridge for at least an hour. For the courgette oil, heat a dash of olive oil in a pan and gently fry the courgette cubes. Add the rest of the olive oil and leave this to simmer on a low heat for half an hour. Strain the oil. Let the olive oil and the courgette cubes cool in separate bowls.

Pour a layer of courgette oil on the gelatinised mousse. Put a few courgette cubes on small spoons and balance these on top of the glasses.

MEAT IN A GLASS

SMOKED TURKEY WITH A MANGO AND PORT SALSA

SERVES 8

Cut half of the turkey filet into small cubes and the other half in thin slices. Mix the turkey cubes, the mango and cucumber with the capers, the chilli pepper and the spring onion. Whisk the port, lemon juice and olive oil into a smooth dressing and season with salt. Stir the dressing and coriander through the mango mixture. Let the mixture infuse for 30 minutes.

Divide the mango and port salsa over the glasses and put 2–3 slices of turkey on top. Garnish with a bit of witlof leaf, some mango slices, rocket (arugula) and a sprig of coriander (optional).

150 g (5 oz) smoked turkey fillet
1 small, ripe mango finely diced
¼ small cucumber, finely diced
1 tbsp capers, washed
½ small chilli pepper, deseeded and finely chopped
½ spring onion, finely chopped
1 tbsp white port
1 tbsp lemon juice
1 tbsp olive oil
1 tbsp coriander, finely chopped

ROAST BEEF WITH GREEN ASPARAGUS AND PARMESAN

SERVES 8

Sprinkle the roast beef with salt and pepper. Melt the butter and olive oil in a pan and brown the roast beef on all sides. Cook off the beef in a oven preheated to 180°C (350°F) for 20 minutes. Let the roast beef cool down completely and then cut it into thin slices.

Cut the asparagus into pieces of 2–3 cm (¾–1 in) and stir in the pine nuts and Parmesan. Build up layers of roast beef slices and asparagus mixture in the glasses. Garnish with some frisee lettuce, Parmesan, wild asparagus and/or green asparagus.

150 g (5 oz) roast beef
25 g (¾ oz) butter
2 tbsp olive oil
1 bunch of green baby asparagus, blanched
2 tbsp pine nuts, roasted
2 tbsp Parmesan, grated

ASPARAGUS CREAM WITH HAM JELLY

SERVES 8

Peel, top and tail the asparagus. Cook them in salted water for 15 minutes. Drain the asparagus and retain the cooking liquid. Puree the asparagus in a food processor or with a blender. Soak the gelatine leaves in a large bowl of water for 10 minutes.

Heat 150 ml (5 fl oz) of the cooking liquid in a pan. Add the stock cube and the 2 squeezed gelatine leaves and stir until these have dissolved. Mix the liquid through the asparagus puree and let this cool down.

Cut the ham into small pieces. Spoon the cream and half the ham pieces through the asparagus mousse and season with salt and pepper. Divide the asparagus mousse over the glasses. Put the *amuses* in the fridge to set.

Heat up another 150 ml (5 fl oz) of the asparagus liquid and dissolve the remaining 2 gelatine leaves. Stir in the rest of the ham pieces and leave to cool down. Stir occasionally. As soon as the ham jelly starts to set, spoon it over the asparagus mousse. Put the mousse and jelly back in the fridge to set completely. Garnish the amuses with halve an asparagus tip, some chervil, shiso cress and chives (optional).

500 g (17½ oz) asparagus
4 gelatine leaves
1 stock cube
1 thick slice of ham
200 ml (7 fl oz) whipped cream

VEAL LIVER MOUSSE WITH RAISINS

SERVES 8

Rinse the liver and tap dry with some kitchen paper. Melt the butter in a pan and brown the liver on both sides. Let the meat cook gently for another 8 minutes. Deglaze with the cognac. Puree the liver in a food processor or with a blender, and strain through a sieve.

Soak the gelatine leaves in a large bowl of water for 10 minutes. Heat the cream, squeeze out the gelatine leaves and dissolve them in the warm cream. Stir in the vegetable broth, veal liver puree and two-thirds of the raisins. Season with salt and pepper. Divide the mixture over the glasses. Put the *amuses* in the fridge to set. Garnish them with the rest of the chopped raisins (optional).

300 g (10½ oz) veal liver, rinsed and cut into pieces
1 tbsp butter
dash of cognac
2 gelatine leaves
100 ml (3½ fl oz) whipping cream
100 ml (3½ fl oz) vegetable stock (fresh or made from a stock cube)
25 g (¾ oz) raisins

FILO PASTRY STICKS WITH PARMA HAM

SERVES 8

Brush the melted butter over the sheet of filo pastry and fold over. Brush with the melted butter again and fold over again. Brush the pastry with butter a last time.

Brush on a thin layer of pesto and sprinkle over the Parmesan. Cut the filo pastry into 8 long strips and lay down a strip of Parma ham next to it.

Roll up the pastry and ham together, forming a sprial. Brush the spirals with some melted butter.

Transfer the spirals to a greased baking tray. Bake them in an oven, preheated to 200°C (400°F), until they are golden brown and crispy. Put a filo stick into each glass or present them together in a large glass. You can also bake the filo sticks without the meat, and wrap this around after baking.

1 sheet of filo pastry, defrosted
25 g (¾ oz) melted butter
2 tbsp red pesto
2 tbsp Parmesan, grated
8 thin slices of Parma ham

DUCK RILLETTES WITH FIGS

SERVES 8

Heat the goose fat in a pan and sauté the onion for 2–3 minutes. Add the pork belly and brown this until all the fat has melted. Only then add the duck and the figs. Let this cook for a few minutes. Add the thyme, bay leaf, the cloves and nutmeg, and deglaze with the cognac, wine and water. Season with salt and pepper.

Put the lid on the pan and let stew on a low heat for 2–3 hours. All the liquid should be evaporated. The meat should be very soft now and you should be able to stir it apart with a fork. Let the mixture cool down a bit and divide it over the glasses. Garnish the *amuses* with a strip of celery, Granny Smith, parsley and fig.

2 tbsp goose fat

1 small onion, shredded

200 g (7 oz) pork belly, finely chopped

200 g (7 oz) duck fillet, finely chopped

75 g (2½ oz) dried figs, finely chopped

1 sprig of thyme

1 bay leaf

2 cloves

a pinch of nutmeg

a measure of cognac

100 ml (3½ fl oz) white wine

100 ml (3½ fl oz) water

MARINATED BEEF FILLET WITH SOY AND SESAME

SERVES 8

Sprinkle the beef fillet with salt and pepper. Mix up the ginger syrup, soy sauce, lemon juice and oyster sauce and marinate the beef for at least an hour. After 30 minutes, mix everything up.

Remove the beef from the marinade and pat dry with some kitchen paper. Reduce the marinade to a sticky sauce and leave to cool. Finely slice the beef and add as much of the marinade sauce and sesame seeds to make it nice and creamy. Whisk up the wasabi and mayonnaise.

Divide the beef fillet over the glasses, add a dollop of wasabi mayonnaise and garnish each *amuse* with some sesame seeds, a strip of fennel and some pea sprouts (optional).

300 g (10½ oz) fresh beef fillet

2 tbsp ginger syrup

2 tbsp soy sauce

2 tbsp lemon juice

1 tbsp oyster sauce

1 tbsp sesame seeds, roasted

a dash of wasabi

1 tbsp mayonnaise

1 tbsp sesame seeds, roasted

FISH IN A GLASS

KING CRAB SALAD WITH LAVENDER MAYONNAISE

SERVES 8

1 tbsp dried edible lavender
 flowers
1 tsp icing sugar
50 ml (1¾ fl oz) vinegar
2 egg yolks
1 tsp mustard
200 ml (7 fl oz) oil
250 g (9 oz) king crabs, finely
 chopped
1 parboiled potato, finely diced
1 spring onion, shredded
2 tbsp dill, finely chopped

Put the lavender flowers, icing sugar and vinegar in a pan and let this infuse on a low heat. Let the sauce cool down and strain through a sieve. Beat the egg yolks, mustard and cooled lavender vinegar with a blender. Slowly add the oil until the desired consistency. Season with salt and pepper.

Mix up the crab, potato and spring onion and add as much of the lavender mayonaise until you get a smooth salad.

Divide the crab salad over the glasses. Garnish the *amuses* with a dollop of lavender mayonnaise and, if desired, fresh lavender flowers, wild asparagus and chives.

Avocado mousse with shrimp and grapefruit

SERVES 8

1 yellow grapefruit
1 ripe avocado
2 tbsp sour cream
2 dried chilli peppers, crumbled
1 tomato, skinned and deseeded,
  diced
2 tbsp chives, finely chopped
100 g (3½ oz) shrimp (prawn)

Peel the grapefruit and remove any white membranes. Cut the wedges in between the membranes and catch any juice that comes out. Cut half the grapefruit into pieces.

Peel the avocado. Remove the stone and finely dice the avocado. Stir in the grapefruit juice.

Puree half the avocado with the grapefruit juice, the sour cream and chilli pepper in the food processor or with a blender. Divide the mixture over the glasses.

Mix up the rest of the avocado, tomato, grapefruit cubes, chives and shrimp. Divide this over the avocado mousse. Garnish the amuses with the rest of the grapefruit wedges and some chives (optional).

SMOKED EEL WITH CUCUMBER JELLY AND CRÈME

SERVES 8

½ cucumber
1 gelatine leaf
200 g (7 oz) freshly smoked eel
4 tbsp crème fraîche
1 tbsp taragon, dill and parsley,
  finely chopped

Grate the cucumber over a bowl to retain the juice. Season the juice with salt and pepper. Transfer the grated cucumber to a colander to drain off. Soak the gelatine leaf in a large bowl of water for 10 minutes.

Bring the cucumber juice to the boil and let it reduce down to 160 ml (5½ fl oz). Squeeze out the gelatine leaf and dissolve it in the cucumber juice. Pour it into a cold bowl and let it cool down and thicken.

Clean the eel and pull the meat off the bones. Finely dice the fish meat. Whip up the crème fraîche, stir in the herbs and season with salt and pepper.

Divide the grated cucumber over the glasses. Fill up the glasses with eel cubes and pour over some of the thickened cucumber jelly. Put the *amuses* in the fridge to let them set. Spoon over a dollop of crème fraîche and garnish the amuses with shiso cress (optional).

SCALLOPS WITH LEMONGRASS AND LEMON BUTTER

SERVES 8

2 sticks of lemongrass
100 g (3½ oz) butter
1 tbsp Thai fish sauce
zest and juice of ½ lime
½ small chilli pepper, finely
  chopped
16 fresh scallops
1 tbsp coriander, finely chopped

Cut the ends of the lemon grass and remove the tough outer leaves. Finely chop the rest of the lemongrass.

Melt the butter in a pan and add the chopped lemongrass, fish sauce, lime zest and juice and the chilli pepper. The butter should just have melted. Make sure it doesn't turn brown! Warm up the mixture for 1–2 minutes. Take the pan off the heat and let the butter cool down (it shouldn't go hard). The butter will infuse with all the flavours.

Arrange the scallops in an oven-proof dish and spoon over the butter. Put them under the grill for 1–2 minutes, turn the scallops and grill them again for 1–2 minutes.

Add 2 scallops to each glass, spoon over some butter and sprinkle with coriander. You can also skewer the scallops on a stick of lemon grass. Garnish the *amuses* with a witlof leaf, a green asparagus and sage.

COD TAPENADE WITH SOLDIERS

SERVES 8

*500 ml (17½ fl oz) fish stock (fresh
  or made from a stock cube)*
300 g (10½ oz) cod fillet
4 tbsp olive oil
½ tin of achovy fillets in oil
1 clove of garlic, cut into pieces
200 g (7 oz) black olives, stoned
2 tbsp capers, drained
4 slices of white bread
1 lemon

Bring the fish stock close to the boil and add the cod. Poach the cod for 5 minutes. Turn the fish over and poach for another 5 minutes. Take the fish out of the pan and let it drain off.

Heat the olive oil in a pan and add the anchovy fillets. Let the anchovy soften for 8–10 minutes.

Pull the cod apart and puree the fish in the food processor or with a blender. Add the anchovy and the oil, garlic, olives and capers. Puree everything again until you have a fine tapenade. Season the tapenade with salt and pepper.

Toast the bread and cut it into strips. Divide the tapenade over the glasses and dip 1 or 2 soldiers into each glass. Squeeze some lemon juice into each glass. Garnish the glasses with small tomatoes and frisee lettuce (optional).

TROUT RILLETTES WITH GRANNY SMITH

SERVES 8

4 tbsp olive oil
125 g (4 oz) smoked trout
1 Granny Smith apple
1 tbsp lemon juice
2 tbsp crème fraîche
2 tbsp chives, finely chopped

Heat the olive oil in a pan and add the trout. Let the fish warm through for 1–2 minutes and turn over. Heat the other side for 1–2 minutes as well. Mash up the trout and the oil with a fork and let it cool down.

Cut the apple into quarters. Remove the core, finely dice the apple and stir through the lemon juice.

Spoon half the apple cubes, the crème fraîche and the chives through the trout and season with salt and pepper.

Divide the trout rillettes over the glasses and spoon over the rest of the apple cubes. Garnish the *amuses* with a slice of Granny Smith apple, some sage, small tomatoes, beetroot sprouts and soldiers (optional).

MUSSELS IN MUSSEL-SAFFRON JELLY

SERVES 8

500 g (17½ oz) mussels in the shell
2 tbsp olive oil
1 bag of soup vegetables
dash of white wine
a few saffron threads
3 gelatine leaves

Rinse the mussels under the cold tap. Debeard the mussels and throw away any broken and opened mussels. Heat the olive oil in a pan and sauté the soup vegetables for 2 minutes, continuously stirring. Add a pinch of salt and the wine and add the rinsed mussels. Put the lid on the pan and let the mussels cook for 10 minutes until they open up. Throw away any mussels that are still closed. Use a slotted spoon to take the mussels out of the pan and let them cool down a bit. Remove the mussels from their shell and put them in a bowl in the fridge for now.

Strain the cooking liquid. Bring 250 ml (9 fl oz) back to the boil with the saffron. Let the liquid simmer for 10 minutes. Soak the gelatine leaves in a large bowl of water for 10 minutes.

Remove the pan from the heat and add the squeezed gelatine leaves. Strain the cooking liquid again. Let the jelly firm up until it is slightly wobbly. Divide the mussels over the glasses and pour over the mussel-saffron jelly. Put the glasses in the fridge to set. Garnish them with mustard mayonnaise and shiso cress (optional).

DESSERT IN A GLASS

YOGHURT CREAM WITH STRAWBERRY ESPUMA

SERVES 8

Beat the yoghurt and sugar into an airy mass and add the cream. Divide the yoghurt over the glasses. Cut 50 g (1¾ oz) strawberries into small pieces and scatter them over the yoghurt. Put the *amuses* in the fridge for now.

Puree the rest of the strawberries with 50 ml (1¾ fl oz) water and put aside. Cook the rest of the water (50 ml/1¾ fl oz) and the sugar into a syrup. Soak the gelatine leaf in a large bowl of water for 10 minutes. Squeeze out the gelatine leaves and dissolve them in the syrup. Let the syrup cool down slightly. Mix in the strawberry puree.

Spoon the mixture into a piping bag with a ridged tip. Pipe the mixture onto the strawberries. If you don't have a piping bag, you can use the blender to mix everything together and spoon a dollop onto the strawberries. Add a strawberry as decoration.

200 g (7 oz) Greek yoghurt
60 g (2 oz) caster (superfine) sugar
150 g (5 oz) whipped cream
250 g (9 oz) strawberries
100 ml (3½ fl oz) water
50 g (1¾ oz) sugar
1 gelatine leaf

FRUIT SOUP WITH SORBET AND RED FRUIT

SERVES 8

Puree most of the fruit (keep some apart for decoration) with the icing sugar and a few mint leaves in a food processor or with a blender.

Divide the fruit soup over the glasses and add a small scoop of sorbet ice-cream.

Garnish the *amuses* with the fruit. Cut any larger bits of fruit into smaller pieces.

You can also use a mint leaf as extra garnish.

250 g (9 oz) mixed red fruit (raspberry, strawberry, currants etc.), rinsed
50 g (1¾ oz) icing sugar
a few sprigs of mint
8 small scoops of lemon, raspberry or strawberry sorbet ice-cream

FROSTY IRISH COFFEE

SERVES 8

Whisk together the cream, whisky, coffee and icing sugar. Spoon it into a whipped cream dispenser with gas cartridge. Put it in the fridge for at least an hour.

Shake and squeeze the Irish coffee foam into the glasses. Sprinkle over some cocoa powder and coffee beans and grated white chocolate (optional).

270 ml (9½ fl oz) whipping cream
1 measure of Irish whisky
200 ml (7 fl oz) strong coffee
4 tbsp icing sugar
1 tsp cocoa powder, sieved
24 coffee beans
white chocolate, grated

WHITE AND DARK CHOCOLATE MOUSSE WITH CHERRIES

SERVES 8

Melt the milk or dark chocolate and white chocolate separately, in a bain marie. Whip the cream and beat the egg whites, separately, into stiff peaks.

Stir in the dark chocolate through half the egg whites. Stir in half the whipped cream.

Stir the white chocolate through the other half of the egg whites and add the rest of the whipped cream.

Divide the dark chocolate mousse over the glasses. Fill them up just below the halfway mark. Fill them up to the top with the white chocolate mousse. Put the glasses in the fridge to set. If the dark chocolate mousse is very thin, let it set in the fridge first before adding the white chocolate mousse. Add a cherry on top (optional).

75 g (2½ oz) milk or dark chocolate

90 g (3 oz) white chocolate

300 g (10½ oz) whipping cream

2 egg whites

8 cherries (with stalks)

PINEAPPLE GRANITA WITH MINT AND CHILLI PEPPERS

SERVES 8

Cut the skin off the pineapple and remove any pips. Cut the pineapple into wedges, removing the core, and cut into smaller pieces. Puree the pineapple pieces in a food processor or with a blender. Bring the puree to the boil, together with the mint, chilli peppers, the water and the sugar. Keep stirring to let the sugar dissolve. Let the mixture cool down and mix in the Malibu (optional).

Pour the mixture into a large container, cover it and put it in the freezer for 2 hours. Take the container out of the freezer. Mash up with a fork and put back into the freezer. Let the ice-cream freeze for another 2 hours, mashing it up every half hour.

Spoon the granita into the glasses. Garnish the *amuses* with a strip of fresh pineapple and cape gooseberry (physalis).

½ pineapple
4 sprigs of mint, leaves only
½ red chilli pepper, deseeded, finely chopped
½ green chilli pepper, deseeded, finely chopped
300 ml (10½ fl oz) water
115 g (4 oz) caster (superfine) sugar
a dash of Malibu (optional)

YOGHURT PANNA COTTA WITH WHITE CHOCOLATE AND RASPBERRIES

SERVES 8

Soak the gelatine leaves in a large bowl of water for 10 minutes. Bring the cream to the boil together with the chocolate and sugar. Keep stirring until the sugar has dissolved. Make sure the cream does not get too warm. Take the pan off the heat. Squeeze out the gelatine leaves and dissolve them in the cream mixture. Pour the mixture into a cold bowl and let it cool and thicken.

Stir up the yoghurt and add the cream mixture. Divide this over the glasses and put them in the fridge to set.

Cut the lemon half into 8 halved slices. Keep the other lemon half in one piece. Squeeze the lemon and stir through the honey. Gently stir in the raspberries. Scoop the raspberries and sauce over the panna cotta. Garnish the *amuses* with the lemon slices.

3 gelatine leaves

125 ml (4 fl oz) whipping cream

75 g (2½ oz) white chocolate

75 g (2½ oz) sugar

300 g (10½ oz) Greek yoghurt

1 lemon

4 tbsp runny honey

50 g (1¾ oz) raspberries

STRAWBERRY AND ORANGE SORBET WITH CANDIED CITRUS FRUIT

SERVES 8

Bring the water and sugar to the boil in a pan. Keep stirring until the sugar has dissolved. Divide the sugar water over three bowls.

Add the orange juice to the first bowl and the lemon juice to the second bowl. Make sorbet ice-cream from both mixtures in an ice-cream maker. Store the sorbet in the freezer.

Pour the third batch back into the pan, add the orange, lemon and lime peel and simmer for 30 minutes. Let the mixture cool down.

Peel the orange and cut out the wedges in between the membranes. Cut the wedges into smaller pieces. Cut the strawberries into small pieces. Mix them with the orange and divide over the glasses. Spoon over a spoonful of candied citrus peel. Spoon a scoopful of strawberry sorbet and orange sorbet into each glass.

Garnish the *amuses* with freshly grated orange, lemon and lime peel (optional).

450 ml (15 fl oz) water
180 g (6 oz) sugar
150 ml (5 fl oz) fresh orange juice
150 ml (5 fl oz) fresh strawberry juice
peel of 1 orange, 1 lemon and 1 lime
1 orange
8 strawberries

Index of recipes

G

H

I

K

L

M

O